how

it happened

PAMELA BROWN

ISBN: 978-0-578-75278-5

Preface

There is an unspoken rule within the African-American community that mental health is not discussed. It is generally understood that if someone is suffering from a mental illness, they are expected to handle it quickly and quietly. Furthermore, there is a stigma placed upon those who seek help from professionals – both they and their family humiliated and shamed. Thus, it is extremely rare for African-Americans to voluntarily seek any kind of treatment.

This tenet has held true in my own family, which has suffered from such debilitating diseases as ADHD, anxiety disorder, eating disorder, manic depression, and severe clinical depression. Undiagnosed and untreated, these illnesses have taken a hefty toll upon the members of my family.

This collection of poetry chronicles my personal descent into severe depression, and the struggle to find my way out. Written in darkness, these poems illuminate my path to the light.

Contents

how it began

I watch the
years pass...

Beauty and Beast

She lied.

But it was more than a dirty little secret

shoveled under the rug,

or a skeleton in the closet

dressed as a fib in disguise.

This was an ugly black truth thrown forth

with bloody spite.

A deep dark sin that reached out and grabbed

his palpitating heart with eager malice.

More than joy at the thought of the blood

jetting forward from his broken, dying heart.

This was sweet iniquity,

with bliss on the side.

This was her passion,

her reason for living, her life,

her only moments of delight

in this desolate wasteland

where a world used to lie-

now only scattered debris of opportunity remain.

And he begs.

Oh, how pitifully he begs.

He begs, he pleads, and he cries.

But her face, devoid of any

compassion or sympathy for others,

will not give in.

She is a deity; she is a fiend.

She is a memory of what once was

and what could have been.

His wounded heart can only imagine.

His wounded heart can only dream.

Mother

I don't think I ever gave you enough credit.

How could you raise a daughter

when you never had a mother?

How could you teach me things

that you were never taught yourself?

Bullets

My tongue will be still each day

from early eve 'til late morn,

waiting to take my cue from you.

I'll speak neither crude nor fair

until I see what pleases your heart,

cause I've found that you'll kill

with words so fierce and deadly

should someone speak before you start.

Give me the word today.

I'll speak what you wish

but you must tell me what to say.

What's in your heart today?

Tell me what you wish.

I will not fight it. I will obey.

Bullets are heavy when delivered with a meaningful heart,

your meaningful heart,

you're mean.

Emotional Terrorism

If you walk on eggshells

in your own home,

then you're never really at home.

When You Hate Me

If you hate me now,
then so be it,
so be it.

I have held my piece
and hidden my heart
to the point where I have lost myself.

And if that's not enough to satisfy you,
if that's not enough to pacify you,
there is nothing more I can do.

So if you hate me now,
then so be it,
so be it.

I hid inside this silent shell,
and uttered what I thought you wanted to hear,
and became what I thought you would hold dear.

So if you hate me now,
then so be it,
so be it.
I have nothing left to give.

Grandma

What was wrong with you?

Why were you so mean?

You went for the jugular every time,

as though you knew no other way to survive.

Tomorrow

Alleged prosecuted queen.

First sorrow, now your soul's missing.

Just yesterday your heart was free.

Makes you wonder who's praying.

Tell the neighbors;

      tell them that he's gone.

Tell the press;

      tell them that he's done you wrong.

You'll face tomorrow with a sadness.

Bless this holy sanctified region,

where insults fly without reason.

Hypocrisy makes the heart grow strong,

and makes for easy living.

Bedraggled mistreated old king.

Your struggles left your soul unclean.

What you're looking for isn't there to see,

but keep on searching.

Tell the neighbors;

       tell them how she's lost.

Tell the press;

       tell them how she always fought.

You'll face tomorrow with a sadness.

Whispers

Whispers, blown soft as cotton,

past the powerful eardrums.

Soft, soft, soft as cotton,

blowing words past the tongue.

Silence, as thick as cotton,

flowing through the small eardrums.

Thick, thick, thick as cotton,

flowing silence finds its way

through the eardrums.

And not again-

pain inside them,

pain inside the velvet eardrums,

as words infuse inside them,

soft words inside the little eardrums.

Pain, as strong as cotton,

growing inside the delicate eardrums.

Strong, strong, strong as cotton,

growing inside the precious eardrums

with words, quite lewd and rotten,

blown past the whispering tongue.

Sunset

The East lights with an orange fire,

spreading contagiously with pride.

Mother is crying.

The neighborhood children ride their bikes,

skateboards, and scooters.

Mother weeps uncontrollably.

The music of the night

creeps into every home,

and lingers in everyone's ears.

Father waves good-bye.

I sit in my window,

and watch the days end,

and watch the nights grow,

and watch the years pass.

Mother desperately sobs.

I watch the years pass.

[24]

how it was

The loneliness so
intense, so absolute…

Journey

All my life is on trial;

heaven's gate discerning.

And the future can't be found.

Hell is on my journey.

Motivation Destroyed

Lazy mist taking over the brain,

fighting my restraints.

It wanders along through the corridors of my mind,

and ceases to find a place it can hold,

until it reaches my motivational goals.

And when all is said and done,

it's over before it has begun.

Its power has effortlessly won,

and my motivation has gone.

Honesty Gone

So this is really me

and all my hateful deeds.

Where has my honesty gone?

And my faithful depression,

waiting for regression

to return with its blue song.

And if I look within

I will find deeper sins,

hidden in the background.

No matter how I lie

they will remain inside,

waiting to be found.

So where does hatred come from

when I thought I was done?

Why has envy made a return?

At my own suggestion

I push those transgressions

deeper to the back of my mind.

As long as no questions have been asked,

and no judgments have been passed

I can be a saint until the praying is done.

So this is really me

and all my hateful deeds.

Where has my honesty gone?

Revelation

But if I'm broken, there's a reason.

Surely I started whole.

Somewhere along the line

I took a pounding to my soul.

The Trouble With Being Your Own Therapist

is that you're never properly diagnosed.

Is this depression?

Anxiety?

Am I socially awkward, or is this social anxiety?

What's the difference, please?

Love Is A Battlefield

They say love is a battlefield.

I don't know anything about that.

But I do know that silence is a battlefield-

overwhelming, crippling solitude

that stifles you from the inside,

the loneliness so intense, so absolute.

I know what that is like.

Questions

Why can't I feel

the way others feel –

hurt, joy, sorrow, fear?

Why don't I cry at the appropriate time?

What's wrong with me?

Waters of Wisdom

Blisters, lies, and distortions

under the mirror of my contentment.

There is no cover like raw emotion

to change appearances of true resentment.

Blisters, lies, and distortions

are the epitome of my existence.

Beneath the cover girl contortion

resides an enemy showing persistence,

and there is a line between our divisions

that is blurring away in my head.

I am wading in waters of wisdom,

but never receiving a vision.

I am bathing in my own pretensions,

making all of the wrong decisions.

It's not helping to think I'm a victim,

though it may be the truth.

It's not helping to voice my opinion,

though there is nothing left to lose.

It's not helping to hope

there is a rescuer coming to my defense.

I'm still unsure if there is a remedy.

The possibilities are fading fast.

I said that I would remain undefeated,

never surrender to fear.

But maybe I retreated from the battle

just when victory was near.

Blisters, lies, and distortions

are the reasons I have bled,

but there is a reason life has been started,

and there is a reason it has not been shed.

I am wading in waters of wisdom,

but never receiving a vision.

I am praying for someone to listen,

and maybe replace what is missing.

I am wasting away from derision-

ignoring accolades, hearing dissension.

I am bathing in my own pretensions,

making all of the wrong decisions.

I am hating my heart for its distance-

tossing out hope before it has come.

Just Wondering

When will I find my voice –

      age 35?

      48?

      50?

When will I find me?

Or rather,

when will I be satisfied

with the person that I see?

Depression

Crying and not knowing exactly why.

Just knowing that everything hurts inside,

and wishing that it were a physical pain

so that aspirin could make everything good again.

But worst of all

is having to lie with a smile,

so that no one knows that you are dying inside.

An Angry Heart

I fear this condition has advanced

to a terminal feeling.

I see the way things have circumstanced

their way into my being.

I fear I've been lost to an angry heart,

helplessly lost to vengeful thoughts.

I fear that reason has given in to noise,

and now it's fading rapidly.

And the sanity that seemed to possess this voice

has dimmed to catastrophe.

I fear I've been lost to an angry heart,

helplessly lost to vengeful thoughts.

The reason that I blame is a memory long gone.

And the guilty name doesn't matter,

because it seems that the matter

really wasn't the force

that broke down my heart.

All Over Again

It's coming on strong,

and I can feel it everywhere.

This dreadful emotion is invading,

taking up space,

forcing me to betray the promises I made

to myself.

All over again.

Rejection

It isn't really self-pity,

though I am well acquainted

with his penetrating song.

Not quite disappointment,

although the tendrils of her brunette curls

lick upon the edges,

teasing for a slit in my armor.

But oddly enough, even this cannot be dredged up.

Perhaps upon reflection,

time wasted in dejection,

the numbing sedative of anger will emerge

to suppress this aggravated pain.

But no,

none of the predictable elements of despair

seem to be located anywhere.

Instead,

most bewildering,

is an infusion of hopelessness and terror

resonating through the core

of a once so confident being,

a loss of certainty when confronted with reality.

Brushed Aside

It doesn't seem to work that way

no matter how I cry and pray.

It doesn't seem to come that way anymore.

How I disregarded

all the warning signs along the way,

denying and lying and pretending

I knew the best route to take.

But pride I see

has betrayed me,

and left me in this sad and pitiful state.

And now that I need it,

I must force feed it.

Because it doesn't come that way,

for I have too far strayed.

Now it doesn't come that way anymore.

Nothing

Has it gone -

drifted away like the fickle breeze

that brushes over my skin

on a cool autumn day?

Has it really gone?

Under-appreciated and entirely misused,

has it abandoned me?

I lived with it for such a very long time,

using and abusing it for my own peace of mind.

I treasured it only when it pleased me to.

And now in hindsight,

I see so clearly why it took flight.

Now what will I do with it gone?

Thoughts of You

Thoughts of you

scatter in my mind,

linger in the recesses -

an all-encompassing void

filled with memories so divine.

Pressing through time.

Pressing through my soul.

Thoughts of you

run deep inside

and cover my heart

with meaningful sighs,

whilst I gather these thoughts,

gather them near

[48]

and covetously hold them so dear.

Thoughts of you

pass slowly

and wilt away with time.

They leave my mind a flowerbed

of lifeless flowers,

asphyxiated from the weeds.

And thoughts of you

float away

with the September breeze.

Evacuation

Break this amendment.

Change the life I've adopted,

I've proclaimed,

and open the door

that will bring me out of chains,

out of my bondage.

The misery I've grown to know

is fighting for my life -

the worst things unsealed

to bind my broken hands.

Falter

Once upon my days gone by

I thought I would give in.

Vanquished to my hole inside,

my heart became too thin.

Then as the hope began to die

within my lonely den,

somewhere afar a light did shine

and illuminated within.

As I slowly found my voice,

I dreamt what could have been.

I longed to have again the choice

to live the life I had envisioned.

And nothing hurts quite like divorce

[51]

from an unrealized dream,

but once impressed upon my force

I relinquished the fantasy.

Now as the days begin to fade

and moonlight lingers by,

for something more I've searched and prayed

to fill the void in my life.

Remembering times when plans were laid,

and I was reaching for the sky,

but residual scars produced a shade,

and now I cannot see so high.

Once upon my days gone by

I thought I would give in,

then somewhere afar a light did shine

and illuminated within.

how it goes

I'm finally strong
enough to do myself some good
this time...

Theory of Doubt

Eyes feel terribly shut; squint for clarity.

Impressing upon my being

the astounding severity-

desperate need for salvation.

If passion is alternating,

is this postulating?

Pompous moral isolation?

Grappling blindly through light

while inside is decaying.

There's a theory of doubt

supplanting positive assurance

of blessed certainty,

highlighting an extraordinary need for mercy.

Dust and Ash

It's down inside me,

building in strength,

developing allies,

gathering its reserves.

And every image I see

sways me ever the more,

lending heart to the truth,

or rejuvenating my foe.

What happened to the love of days ago-

the delight of the law?

How can such confidence stumble and fall?

Crumbled to dust and ash

under the watchful eye of self-righteousness.

The Furnace

So it is not for me –

this is clear.

But the furnace still burns,

drowning inside.

Barely hidden,

but the memory is blurry.

Was the promise made?

Promises made are promises kept.

But was it a dream entirely?

A sad fantasy?

Still never do tears go unnoticed,

and cast aside are pitiful moments.

Cause there is always more –

other avenues to pursue,

until discontentment cannot be bargained

and heaviness greatly subdued.

God Is Frankenstein

I assumed I was a mistake-

unfeeling, emotionless mistake.

The failed experiment

escaped from God's science lab.

Why else would I be here,

when clearly I don't belong?

But maybe,

maybe

He meant for me to be this way.

Maybe he planned it all along.

Simple Truths

1. I don't have to be as good as everyone else.
   I have to be as good as me.
   Better than me.
   Best as me.

   I wish I had been told this as a little girl.

Just Because

Just because I've never been in love

doesn't mean I don't know what love is.

I've read about it in books.

I've seen it in movies.

Just because I've never felt joy

doesn't mean I don't understand it.

I've heard about it from others.

I've dreamed about it for myself.

Just because I haven't lived

doesn't mean I can't recognize life.

Battered Wings

Broken thunder

bend these battered wings,

crumbling under impressionable things.

Falling, standing, crawling endlessly,

preying upon my wounded ways.

And I am barely stumbling along,

holding shadows just at bay.

Where's the passion?

Where's the memory?

Songs of land flowing with milk and honey?

But there's love brewing

deep inside my veins,

whispering hope to light my way.

This Pain

I'm giving up on this pain.

It's done all its service

and I've decided that it's time.

This loneliness makes me sick

and it's served its purpose,

so I'm setting it free from my mind.

Then I'll finally recover.

I'll feel my heart has been uncovered,

excavated and found.

For everything I've discovered,

I'll be all the wiser

and all the darkness will be over.

I'm going to liberate the rain.

I'm putting it out of my future-

redeem the wrath.

And it should all be a cinch,

cause I'm long overdue for

a day with a clear path.

I'm finally strong enough

to do myself some good

this time.

Too Far Gone

I didn't swear, I didn't weep,

underneath the tower of a new dawn.

Too much to ask

that this turmoil is finally settling.

Beyond the graveyard

of venomous thoughts.

Bewildering that I'm not

too far gone,

beneath the water I've been treading.

But I could not invent the truth,

and I would not pretend to improve,

and still I finally got here.

Broke the surface,

breathing again, breathing again.

Yet it's astounding that I'm not

too far gone,

underneath the pollution I've been inhaling.

Post War

What happens after the war –

when you're scarred and wounded,

and all that you know lies dead around you?

What happens when you're left

standing on the battlefield

with all of your past burnt to ashes behind you,

and no one alive to steer or guide you?

What happens then?

What happens when you fought the battle

alone in silence,

and cried to yourself in private?

I survived the war,

but where do I go from here?

Just A Memory

I'm not angry anymore.

I'm not depressed anymore.

I'm not even sad or upset.

I'm not bitter.

I'm not lonely.

All of those things that I thought would end me

are just a memory of old poems.

I fought the beast and won

with only scars to prove it was real,

and poetry to show how I healed.

Simple Truths

2. God loved me
   even when no one else did.
   God loved me
   even when I didn't love myself.

   I still struggle to understand this.

Thank You Kat Savage

I thought I wasn't good enough.

There are others so much better.

I thought I should give up.

But you gave me the courage

just to try.

Jesus

I gave my life to Jesus –

it felt like the only thing I have ever

had control over.

I gave my life to Jesus

because I wasn't doing anything

with it anyway.

I gave my life to Jesus

since I had made such a mess of it myself,

I figured I'd let Him have a try.

I gave my life to Jesus,

hoping He could save me.

About the Author

Pamela Brown lives in Port St. Lucie, Florida. She is an audiobook narrator and a tutor, who spends her free time reading, writing, and thinking about reading and writing.

Follow Pamela on social media:

Twitter - @pnicolebrown1

Tumblr – theliteratelife